Sharks

Experts on child reading levels
have consulted on the level of text and
concepts in this book.

At the end of the book is a "Look Back and Find" section
which provides additional information and encourages
the child to refer back to previous pages
for the answers to the questions posed.

Angela Grunsell trained as a teacher in 1969.
She has a Diploma in Reading and Related Skills
and for the last five years has advised London
teachers on materials and resources.

Published in the United States in 1985 by
Franklin Watts, 387 Park Avenue South, New York, NY 10016

© Aladdin Books Ltd/Franklin Watts

Designed and produced by
Aladdin Books Ltd, 70 Old Compton Street, London W1

ISBN 0-531-10025-1

Printed in Belgium

FRANKLIN · WATTS · FIRST · LIBRARY

Sharks

by
Kate Petty

Consultant
Angela Grunsell

Illustrated by
Karen Johnson

Franklin Watts
New York · London · Toronto · Sydney

Did you know that the biggest sharks of all are quite harmless? A Whale Shark is bigger than a bus but it only eats tiny fish.
The Dogfish is the littlest shark.

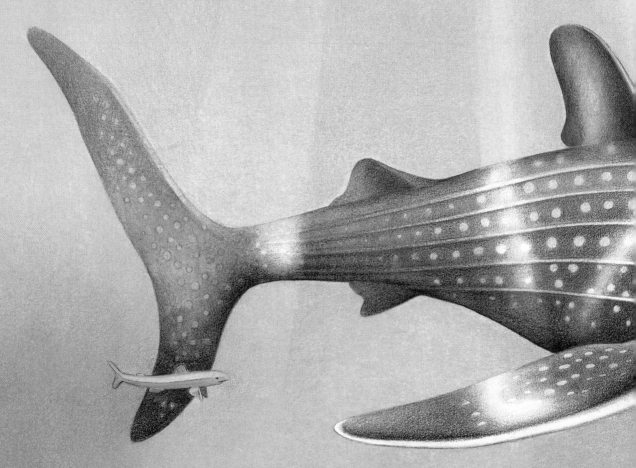

Sharks have swum the oceans of the world
for 350 million years.
They are the largest fish in the sea.
There are 250 different kinds.

Sharks are streamlined for speed. Even a medium-sized one can travel at 22 mph. They thrash their tails to swim along. Their fins keep them upright.

Most sharks have to keep moving,
or they would sink.
Other fish have air bladders which
keep them afloat.

What else makes a shark different from other fish?
Most fish have a bony skeleton (like you do)
but a shark's skeleton is made of gristle.
Its skin is covered in sharp points, like thorns.

The shark's jaw contains many rows of teeth.
As the front ones wear down they are replaced
by the row behind.
One shark might grow 24,000 teeth in ten years!

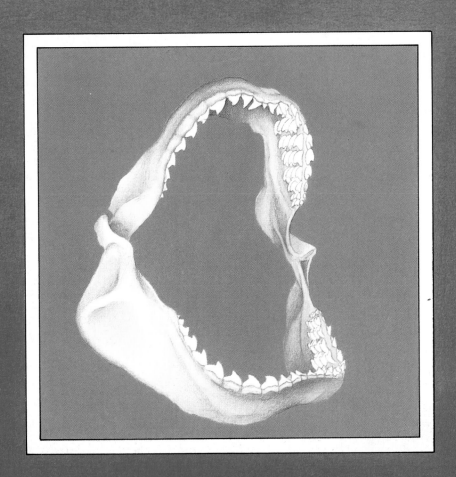

Although sharks are shortsighted this one knew
a wounded whale was near by. It could taste
the blood and feel the vibrations in the water.
It circled the whale and bumped it a few times.

12

Then it came in fast and tore off one huge mouthful after another. Sharks' teeth are for biting, not chewing. Pilot fish and sucker fish called remoras follow the shark for crumbs.

These sharks are feeding on squid. There's plenty for all of them. Some sharks are not fussy about their food. They will eat pigs, dogs, turtles, and even old boots and tin cans!

When a group of sharks pick up the smell
of a wounded creature they go quite crazy.
They rush in to tear at the animal,
often biting each other at the same time.

15

Blue Sharks are about thirteen feet long. They are probably the most common sharks. They will attack people but they usually stay away from the coast.

The Thresher Shark's long tail helps it to hunt fish, but it is harmless to humans. One lash of its tail stuns a fish and sometimes sends it flying straight into the Thresher's mouth!

Can you guess why the Leopard Shark
got its name?
It is only six feet long and not very fierce.
The Leopard Shark is found in California waters.

Tiger Sharks are about ten feet long.
They are extremely dangerous. Their teeth
are curved and razor-sharp. Their mouths
are enormous for the size of their bodies.

The Australian Wobbegong is an unusual shark.
It is hard to see it lying close to the bottom
because it blends in with the seabed.
The frills around its mouth look like seaweed.

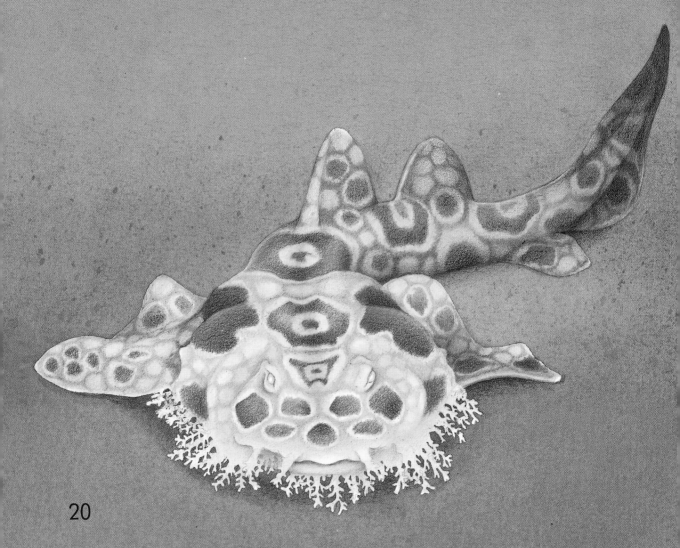

Hammerhead Sharks often hunt in groups.
They are nearly fifteen feet long and very fierce.
Their eyes and nostrils are at either side
of the hammer-shaped head.

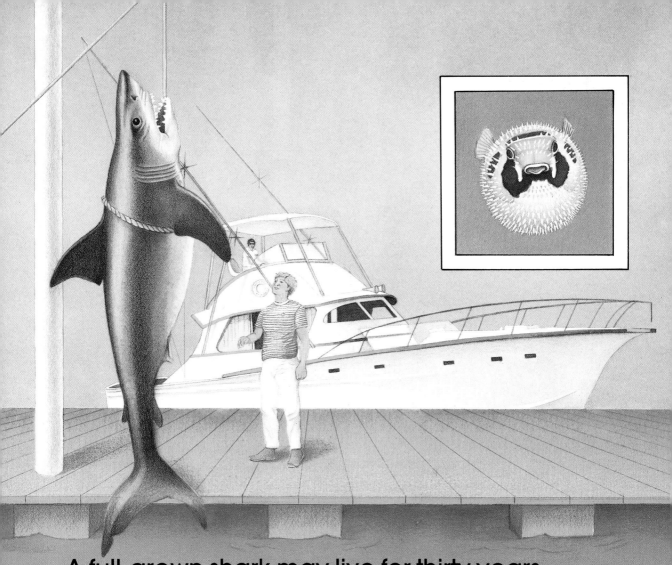

A full-grown shark may live for thirty years.
Humans are their chief enemies.
Fishermen kill sharks to protect their fish.
People hunt them to eat, and for their oil.

Another enemy is the porcupine fish, which swells up in the shark's throat and chokes it. Sometimes a group of dolphins or porpoises might attack a shark, so might a killer whale.

Sharks like warm water and so do bathers.
Shark nets keep the sharks away from beaches.
Although many people come across sharks at sea,
less than a hundred people a year are attacked.

Only a few sharks will even try to attack humans.
Great White Sharks are killers which can grow
up to forty feet.
Usually they live far away from land.

These divers don't want to hurt the sharks. They want to study them. They watch and take photographs. They are trying to mark this one so they can see where it goes.

The divers are brave, but they are ready to
get away quickly if the White-tipped Sharks attack.
Would you like to be with them?

Look back and find

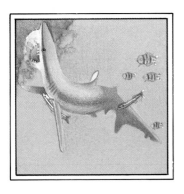

What sort of shark is this?
It is a Blue Shark like the one on page 16.

Why do pilot fish and remoras travel with sharks?
So they can pick up scraps of food. Remoras stick on to the sharks and hitch a ride.

Do you know the name of this shark?

How big is it?
It is twenty feet long.

What does it use its long tail for?

This Wobbegong is nearly six feet long. How does it manage to hide from other fish?

Can all sharks lie still?
No. Most sharks have to keep moving to stay afloat and to be able to get a good supply of oxygen from the water.

Why are these dolphins attacking the shark?
The dolphins have probably got babies and they are trying to keep the shark away.

How do sharks have their babies?
Young sharks hatch from eggs (sometimes before the eggs leave the mother.) They can look after themselves right away.

Do all sharks attack human beings?

What sort of shark is the one in the film *Jaws*?
A Great White Shark like this one.

Do Great White Sharks live close to land?

Why are the divers studying sharks?
Because there are still many things we don't know about them. What else would you like to know?

What is the cage for?
To protect the divers against the sharks.

Index

B   Blue Shark 16, 28

D   divers 26, 29
Dogfish 6
dolphins 23, 29

E   eggs 29
enemies 22, 23

F   feeding 13, 14, 15
fins 8
food 14

G   Great White Shark 25, 29

H   Hammerhead Shark 21

J   jaw 11

L   Leopard Shark 18

P   pilot fish 13, 28
porcupine fish 23
porpoises 23, 29

R   remoras 13, 28

S   skeleton 10
skin 10
speed 8

T   tails 8, 17
teeth 11, 13
Thresher Shark 17, 28
Tiger Shark 19

W   Whale Shark 6
White-tipped Shark 27
Wobbegong 20, 28

PRINTED IN BELGIUM BY

proost

INTERNATIONAL BOOK PRODUCTION